Home, the Farm

Poems by Laurence J. Sasso, Jr.

*To David Dragone
In great appreciation for all you do for poetry!
Laurence J. Sasso, Jr.
June 28, 2023*

Copyright © 2020, Smithfield Publishing Inc.

All rights reserved. Except for brief quotations used for purposes of review, none of this book may be reproduced in any form or by any means without written permission from the publishers.

Published by Greyledge Press,
an imprint of Smithfield Publishing, Inc.
Smithfield, Rhode Island

Other Works by Laurence J. Sasso, Jr.

Is Where The Heart

Is Where the Heart is a collection of short fiction from Rhode Island poet and columnist Laurence J. Sasso, Jr. With a combination of nostalgia, wit, pathos, and grit, the author peels back the bucolic surface of a lively rural community to reveal the inner nature of its inhabitants at their best and their worst.

Dedication

This collection is dedicated to the family whose struggles to tame their resistant farm and orchard land in Rhode Island inspired the poetry. It is for my grandfather Vito P. Sasso, my father Laurence J. Sasso, Sr., my Uncle Anthony R. Stone (née Sasso), my grandmother Adeline L. Sasso, and my mother Phyllis L. Sasso.

Table of Contents

Leaving Italy	1
Planting Apple Trees	2
Under the Belly of the Fordson	4
First Earth, April	8
Food from Home	9
Early Morning, Farmers Market	11
Catholic on the Plow	12
Berry Bush by the Barn Scar	14
No One Forgets the Day	16
Sixty-eight Days Without Rain	19
Favored Place	21
Clearing the Lower Mac Lot, February	23
Walking Beside the Fordson	25
Possible Reasons Why They Didn't Move the Junk Car From the Field	26
Swimming Lesson	28
The Younger Brother Dreams of Trees	30
What Ever Rests?	32
Girl on the Morning Horse	34
Walking Out on Black Ice	36
Once Again April	38
Making Way for the New Orchard	39
Farm Inventory	41
Fire in the Wall	43
Grandfather at Mid-Life	46
Sailing Scythes	49
Under the Black Twig Tree	52

Wet Clarinet	53
Sudden Flare Up	55
Father Eating, 2 a.m.	56
Father Climbs the Sky	59
At Last, Rain	61
Love, Death, a Moment in a Cave	62
The Door Half Open	63
Little Red	65
Seeing the Lion	67
The Backyard in October	69
Late Plans to Escape	71
Morning in the Horse Meadow	72
Checking Out the Old House	74
The Axe and the Apples	76
The Shape of Truth	77
At Work	78
Easy to Lose	79
God's Man Among the MacIntosh	80
Prayer and Maggots	83
Fugue	85
The Swallow in the Silo	89
What Youth	91
Morning Sun Rushes up Across the City	92
Not Often Seen or Found	93
Breaking It	94
Whole Piles of Brush	95
Father's Typical Day	97
Grandfather Kills a Rat by the Barn	98
Fat With Water	100

Why Love is Like the Snow	101
The Blind Orchardist Refuses to Discuss the Day They Burned the Last of His Trees	102
At Father's House	103
Picking Peppers in the Dark, Fall Impending	104
Cold Baptism - Excerpt From The Carpenter Walks	106
Drunk Picker	108
Which is Your Shadow	110
Finding the Algorithm of the Cove	112
Last Mission	114
Night on the Porch	115
The Light Across the Lake	117
Digging Up a Hand	119
Cold November	122
Attributions	i

Acknowledgments

I want to thank the following people:

My daughter Lauryn E. Sasso provided extensive and sustained assistance in formatting, designing, and copy-editing this collection.

Robert J. Oberg contributed editorial advice and insight, especially in regard to the ordering and placement of the poems. His sensitive and close reading of the manuscript was of considerable help. His candor and incisive judgment in the area of prosody was vital.

Ron Scopelliti created the cover from a 1932 photo in the author's private collection. It features (l-r) his father Laurence J. Sasso, Sr. at age 12, his grandfather Vito P. Sasso, and his great-grandfather Antonio Sasso. They are shown with a primitive spray rig used to treat the apple crops against insect and fungus infestations.

Richard Prull's technical skill in enhancing the photo and improving its clarity is greatly appreciated.

Laurence J. Sasso, Jr.
Greenville, Rhode Island

Introduction

> After 34 years on an orchard farm I still feel the surge of spring and in the swelling buds the whole expansion of earth and water and trees. The dark hibernation is seemingly gone forever. Water creatures from old bogs and waterways clack a vociferous repetition. Thus pelted, worn out winter dissolves and seldom reappears in its original form.

My father, Laurence J. Sasso, Sr., wrote the words above on April 4, 1959 in one of the many private daybooks, commonplace books, and diaries he kept during his lifetime.

Born in 1920, he died in in 1995. In between he lived 70 years on the apple farm in Smithfield, Rhode Island which his family had bought in 1925. They took up residence Thanksgiving week of that year.

His entries, written in long-hand, fill numerous journals. They weave together his memories, observations, hopes, diversions, confessions, aspirations, frustrations and, at times, his despair.

It is not surprising to me that he often escaped into the kind of metaphorical reflection quoted above. Poetry, a life-long passion, was for him both a way to cope and a means of transforming to something hopeful the challenging, sometimes soul-crushing work of besting an environment that resisted efforts to tame it.

In his later years, when he could no longer tend the orchards, he wrote and published poems and together we gave readings. For while I had inherited his interest in poetry, I had not followed his calling as an orchardist. My career has been in writing and publishing.

Today I own what remains of the land that once was the Sasso farm, the acres that fed and clothed and sheltered four generations. Like my father, I have lived on this land for most of my days.

In the pages that follow are 68 of my poems selected from my wider body of work. They tell part of the story of what I call *Home, the Farm*.

No finite number of poems could evoke the entire spectrum of any family's enduring struggle to wrest a living and a life from the land. My hope is that the work in the following pages is sufficiently compelling and engaging to give readers a deep and varied enough insight to honor the sacrifice and the commitment of the people whose story they tell.

Laurence J. Sasso, Jr.
2020

Leaving Italy

Flat steel slat, the sun
cuts water, limb, eye of the traveler
there in the fat hot valley of olive trees

The family left the city of Avellino
to ride the boat to America, some
among the Ellis Island millions hungering

Great-grandfather first onto land, opportunity
waiting in Rhode Island where wet hawks
sat above granite and brittle orchards

He would be remembered for silence, a stance
against lonely sky, language broken as ledge,
his future noisy with the strife of survival

Planting Apple Trees

Grandfather's powerful fingers
work among the roots, dark, wet
fertile in their sphagnum pouch.

He picks the right tree
for each hole, matching
imagination against terrain.

This is faith fruit,
trees that won't bear
for another eight or nine years.

His tongue presses his cheek
as if it were looking for light;
he sweats in the May chill.

My father opens the dirt for him,
carving the soil so cleanly
it seems the hole was there before.

They pour water from greasy cans
over the roots and clip the ends
off the longest lateral branches.

It is blue darkness that slows them,
not the weariness of their legs
or satisfaction at what has been done.

Grandmother has given up
calling them to come in and eat.
The dogs have wandered back to the porch.

The idea of apples, not the palpable fruit,
keeps them moving down row after loam-sodden row
as they struggle to make an orchard.

Under the Belly of the Fordson

Under the crucial Fordson
unaware of his godmother
praying over a well,
innocent of agony and the tricks
of maggots under the calyx, hidden
as mud wasps hide in the dome of a bell,
my father learns the names of tools.

The fearsome Fordson, when it runs,
juggles combustion like thunder;
its great iron grouser plate wheels,
built for a Yorkshire ditch,
blueprinted by the same people
who perfected the tank.

But it is standing now,
still as stone, useless
as ledge the glacier laid bare
when it first rolled back the loam
like a thin brown frock over knees all bone.

When the tractor can't move they can't eat.
Handing my grandfather "monkeys"
and the elegant Stilson wrench,
father learns the hierarchy of the parts,
how to tell the oil slinger
from the timing gear,
the way the spindle bushing's meant to clear
the space within the frame
outside the spindle pin.

Washing his hands in gasoline,
his school soft fingers sting.
Under the belly of the Fordson
crying for it to start,
he is new to the country.

He shrinks from the crank.
It can break your arm
quicker than a Belgian's hoof,
but here are more frightening commands.

With shirt sleeve sop
his father wipes the sweat away
and curses the British mechanic
who bolted the head to the block.
Hammering the worn thrust bearing
onto the worn gear flange
he is unconscious of the boy's adjustment,
the family's shock.

His wife in the kitchen
draws a thin stream from the pump,
the rusty plasma of a whitening Eden.

Still the Fordson will not catch.
(Dirt between the stubborn magneto
and the track in the magneto bracket.)

No more apples will get to market
while it sits. Father keeps on,
turning it over and over. At last,
rage spirals backward through the ratcheting,
fracturing kick of the crank.

"Sporcaccione! Bruto! Scarmuccia!
Bastard! What must Italians do to New England?
Dio mio!"

At which raging
my father runs with white eyes
up where there are caves in the hill,
to haunt the moonlight with promises,
willing his shadow to freeze.

While from the dooryard below
the endless stain of America
spreads in all directions
from the dark spot
the tractor marks.

First Earth, April

The first earth of April
fits the shovel like a hand
gripping another hand

Rust on the steel
melts away in the sod
as the soil shines the blade

Just warm enough
to invite the touch
just cold enough to doubt

The land promises life
Yet, life is not the land's
to promise or assure

It is the sun and the seed
that get the final say and we
that get to wait and hope to reap

Food from Home

Polenta the color of fire,
great grandmother paces the kitchen,
corn meal beneath her nails, apple petal
stuck to her cheek.
She is at this farm in America
to feed her daughter and grandchildren
and the muttering son-in-law.
She moves her wooden spoon in a sign of the cross
over the thickening mush.

Wind from the Atlantic
seeps under the window,
loose as a steerage porthole.
It blows out the fire, penetrates
her black godmother shawl,
like "a thousand white needles."
she kisses her crucifix.

Pretense foreign to her as apple sauce,
she can't hide frowns and pain
when the children speak in a language
strange as milkmen and the native grain.

Spoons and fingers mingle
in the platter, red sauce over the food
like a blush on dirty snow.
The family eats. It is a business.

By herself by the window
she sings of the moon and an olive grove,
where the air is warm as blood
and daughters let down their hair to comb.

An ocean too big to cross again
rises on the evening tide
and threatens to overcome her
and this is where she comes to hide,

The odd flower opening in her chest

Early Morning, Farmers Market

Peddler heaven:
the ripe
the red
the bursting blush
the greenest head
paper cups in the truck cab
the grandson asleep on a bale

Dollar bills stuffed
in the overall bib
the early paper
making a fire that
swollen fingers grab for and caress
and – priest like – seem to bless

Hours of waiting,
selling, swapping,
counting stock,
an ache to finish up
to leave
before the sun reveals
the wilt, the waste,
the compost
commerce will create

Catholic on the Plow

Catholic on the plow
Catholic in the loam
the horse rising in offense
to the knifing leaden bit

Wind picks the milkweed
showering the reins
with thistle and dust
closing the eyes of the uncle

New earth opens behind
a furrow of wet soil lips
Ahead is sod tight as thatch
the hillside petering toward the wash

Belts and corsets and linen
blow as sails blow below
on the dooryard laundry line
over ducks and the guinea hen

Hail Marys make the field fertile
Father and his father beside him
fill the rows with pure bred seed,
contrition makes it rain

Darkness draws the trees together
the children cut their laces
leap from the stone into the stream
sheep follow the leader into a blind ravine

The steel of the plow share brightens,
soil buffing it smooth, leaving it clean
The women in the kitchen stop praying
sour as an incense of sweat and lye

A cloud comes down to the absent sister
on the hill behind the house
where, flesh, lacking in granite's grace,
she longs to understand her place

Berry Bush by the Barn Scar

Berry bush by the barn scar
the Germans, who farmed here
before grandfather,
planted better than suspected.
All whetstone business
and uncompromising edges.

Father's father
cleared the dooryard, orchard
and pastures, a farm barber
depilitating the jaw of Rhode Island
ledge that thrust
just under the flesh of his land,
cutting away
Teutonic notions of provision
his Mediterranean eye unpleased
with the cramped order of
the yard.

Spare art his motto,
his sons, his woman
learned the way of blades
and sheared off thorns;
his crews, nephews, cousins,
urban refugees, hugged snaths,

sent scythe knives keening
over acres of the coarse,
slow-yielding dog-like grass,
where the former stewards
let the multiflora rose, fire-like,
go free against the trees.

At bay, apostasy, the weeds
subdued,
subsumed, made way
for apples, other crops,
commerce and the immigrant Italian's
quenching of his want.

Yet root or leaf somehow endured
in some pocket of the rock,
in the manure pit,
the angle of a fence, until
today the berries grow
again around the barn's grown over spot;
the last century's roses wrap and climb
among the derelicts of apple culture,
and wild iris cluster
in the ivy and the grass
where untethered Jerseys
bellowed at the swallows
in the past.

No One Forgets the Day

Rind of sod
curled back
by the knife of wind
dropping
over the cliff
waits for the horse,
the man, the plow

Mother, her brother,
the hens and cow
shudder at the gale
slamming the shutters
on the barn

Somewhere under the loam
she expected to find the gold
America hid from newcomers
or at least money buried
by the suspicious Yankees
who played out the farm
before they sold it to Italians

Every rock pried from the loam
by the men with their crowbars
might be a marker

or shelter for the strong box
she knew she would find

Father and the uncles saw
only work, stone sweat,
early hernias that meant
they'd wear trusses
shaped like gray eggs
smelling bad beneath
the rented suits
at their children's weddings

Whatever is under the dirt
the dirt feeds them, buys their clothes,
fattens the apples, yellows
the squash, and breaks
the tines of the spring tooth harrow

It is the flesh of their world
black or, near the ledge, gray
below the beard of grass
She is content to leave
it to his father, the others
to break it, enter it, spread it
with warm dung,

but always she asks
to look into the furrows first

And no one forgets
the day she slashed
the men with roses,
opening cuts in her husband,
chasing her brothers with a hoe

Until the tears came
undried by the wind,
washing her cheek
as her long body
darkened the sod
where she lay
in the barren lap of the soil
one arm under dirt and grass
clawing the plowed ditch bottom,
cursing the earth
in a language scented with olives,
thickened with fear

Sixty-eight Days Without Rain

So strong is the brush of feathered bone
he doesn't know if it's dream
or drought-inspired madness, apples shriveling
on the dry stick, leaf-yellow limbs,
the birds all gathering on the barn

Outside at night, stamping up plumes
of dust with every staggering step
grandfather prays to the rafters
now full of black, and blacker, birds,
coal black birds, who have moved in
screeching like starving owls,
filling the shelter with the whir
of their beating wings, hundreds
of nocturnal birds, their droppings
falling like the rain that will not come

Afraid to wake the family
father's father stones the nearest one,
swearing in his Italian voice
as they all rise to the ridgepole
gathering into ominous clouds,
the wind from their dark wings
beating down, a hot vortex,
forcing him to lie in the dirt

of the barn's old floor
fighting, crying,
desperate to wake up
or go back to sleep

Favored Place

The birch branch
whipped by wind
bends to slash
through water like a thought
which forms no language

My father and his mother
at this spot
ate lunches of sausage
and sharp cheese,
their own apples and
white milk, warm
and newly suffered
from the cow

In the garden all the
pepper plant ghosts
have rings of ice
around the stem
below the loam,
like penal collars
that keep them
from going off to
die completely

The nearest Italian neighbor
mourns her children
and washes her feet
with lemon water in
the sink before daylight,
prays for happy deaths

But,
sunlight strikes her house
in such a way that time
and pain for a moment
leave no more mark
than the blown birch
left on the lake
No photos exist
and her daughters are gone;
she cannot read or write
The wind gives way
to perfect stillness
slowly, solemn
as her children's tears.

Clearing the Lower Mac Lot, February

Flame rains down
from rotted oak,
old Astrachans,
and dry punk pine.

Father and grandfather
tend the pile of fire
on this Sunday afternoon,
pushing loose branches
into the white pyre
with the limbs of fallen trees.

They crowd brush and embers
back toward the center,
eyes a bright rage of glass,
until at last
their impromptu brooms
burst loudly into flame.

First stunned, then wild
they sweep,
their glowing boughs
erratic in the drifts.

Dark trails of ash
create queer runes,
clotted script
on the blackening snow.

The children race
for the dooryard,
afraid of these men
clearing their orchard with fire,
banging flaming saplings,
while a shower of coals
falls all around them.

Walking Beside the Fordson

Every steel revolution of the dirt-dripping wheel
takes grandfather three steps toward prayer,
father driving the pachyderm tractor,
is measuring furrows for an acre of squash

Loam from this land sifting into his cuffs,
his tongue poking his cheek into the wind,
cursing birds and the fox that watches,
Italy so far from his fingers, his face, lost
in the wake of his ship, his mother's scarf

Street song melodies, dry soil vibrating on the strings
of the mandolin, his uncle dragging him to sing,
but here only the rhythm of the cylinders banging
raw gasoline, red fumes streaming from the stack

The smell of flowers next to a kneeler, stronger than offal,
carpet stains by the oak box imprinted on his memory,
knobbed and swollen old man's hands come to rest
wrapped in rosaries from the first church in Avellino

And the tractor, the awful tractor pulls up the land
Dumps the raw earth back under, ripped by iron cleats
And a walking man demanding it give up its bounty
A fair trade for uprooting a family, planting it here

Possible Reasons Why They Didn't Move the Junk Car From the Field

Inside the inside light
a bulb alive,
a bee, tries flight

The door open like
an arm swung out
in invitation
showing the seat that
rats have tried to eat

It smells like sheep
in the rain, like
the basement of the
empty rotted milking shed

The headlights
broken open like glass flower buds
reveal the pistils the sealed-beam
centers seem

The battery is leaking acid behind
the wheel, the last occupant
of the driver's place

A wild briar is wiring
itself around the
frame, the vicious rose
that time
has made to seem
the blame

Swimming Lesson

Rough as a gravel river,
swim hole in the stream
by the spring lot where
water cold as winter
is bubbling from the earth
in August

Girl and mother
trying to learn
while the men sweat
and mow the angry hay
under the cash fat Baldwin trees

Cream white thighs
wobble in the numbing
current, soft feet reddening
on the shale beneath, the roots
alive as tentacles writhing
out from the undercut bank
to encircle their knees

Poor place to swim
where the cows drink
and the cider pomace
is dumped to rot,

poor place to be
in the mid-day heat

Dripping from each seam
and crevice
they roll onto the dry grass,
pick among sharp stones,
their hands clutching each other,
as they head for the house

Thinking of sweet cheese
and the night
the sad ache of failure
close as the damp curls
on their necks, they
are afraid of the unfamiliar,
rage, so strong
they both start to cry
and she hears
for the first time
her mother curse

The Younger Brother Dreams of Trees

As the cold plaster touches
his back where the bed shirt
rides down, he wakes
wondering if the mosquito
that bites the owl bites him
will he see mice in the dark
or be able to turn his head
all the way around on his neck.

Little by little he warms enough
to sleep again in the white, cold bed,
the ceiling slanting over him
like the ledge across the cranberry bog
where father found the fox
dead with the kits still suckling.

And he dreams of trees,
Gravensteins shaped like camels
and Baldwins big as scaffolds
until he becomes a tree himself,
his hands full of nests and Greenings,
the wind lifting him till it feels
like he will come loose, panic
running down his trunk like fire.

Suddenly ladders stick into him
and men climb up his sides
the whole family tearing parts
away from his limbs, his green leaves,
his best apple flesh, ripped out
the stems still attached to the branch

Praying for salvation
or a storm, he twists
cracking bark, catching spider webs,
milkweed pods, a newspaper
floating over the wall from the road.
He shakes off the dooryard cat
rises at last out of the earth
to stand up on his roots,
run for the woods, faster
than the neighbor's blue tick hounds
until he is flying across the valley,
a tree in the sky high over the orchards
making the rest look up in wonder
at the sight of his wings
full of fresh red apples

What Ever Rests?

Fitting loose like a lit fuse
the flowered vine flames
over the loam

A snake follows the plough
uncoiling along the opening furrow

The former farmer's father's bones
are under the same blanket

At night the stones
heat the moth, mother
the toad, the memory of sun
striving to survive

When the house light goes out
the firefly's code becomes
apparent

Grandfather dreams of Naples,
his family's root moved
North and West three thousand
miles; he jerks in sleep.

In the field, the snake, a curved stick, embrace,
replicate each other's grace

The bones give up another day's
quotient of European matter

An eagle big as an angel
closes a talon on a
soft limb and sways
while the dream is danced
away

In the dark a bridge
of dirt is lapped by waves,
the farmer's wife gets up,
looks out a window
at the land, black as the
unlit mirror in her hand

The dreamer worries through
a cry, a lattice on the
house rattles in the wind
like bone against a piece of tin,
the sounds of time
acculturating kin.

Girl on the Morning Horse

The under-ground stallion
gallops along with the girl
on the wet horse at dawn,
cutting reckless over the meadow,
half up the hill from the house.

Bareback and shoeless and blue
eyed in paint-spattered pants and a bra
she rides a rag line
of tatters and briars
where the men chased
a loose dog
the morning before.

Apple farm wary, our fathers
wake to hoof thrash,
the mane and the girl's hair
lit with small bits of sun
over jewels of dew.

Erect on the morning horse
she is coming straight at them,
crossing the line from pasture
to Baldwin lot orchards,

pumping the reins, rising,
falling with the round back
while under the earth
of the garden, under the corn
the other horse, black, hot,
beats its way
through shale and clay,
stones and loam,
matching the cantering gait above,
fighting to break from the darkness,
come loose from silt and root,
burst from the dirt
to rear up by the girl,
ride with her into the river,
the sun drawing them both
to a place alone,
shaking,
whole.

Walking Out on Black Ice

Like mice
and thin
black water
witch skin
cold as inertia

Undulating under us
like cilia: green weeds
the dog skates sidelong
to rotten ice, barks,
turns back

The current
swings around
the weeds mimic
the current

Stunned-spine fish
float in the water
which is blacker than
the ominous bridge

The weeds stand up
to let it pass

Bubbles like knockwurst
link up beneath
the black glass

The dark pavement
holds together,
cries, the noise
of false agony
groaning over
dead logs and leaves

The current sways
its grass skirt
and writhes

Hair in the nostrils hardens
it is moisture freezing
inside the head

Something deeper in
is fusing
snow swirls out over
open water, goes in.

Once Again April

Limbs are spare, empty
the owl call is mute
soot-stained snow
sits like cuffs of fur
on dark and barren bark

All winter the wind
is loose amid the leafless wood
playing random music
on the gray trees like un-tuned harps,
but in sleep we feel the thaw begin
with melodies and rain

Until, in our last dreams of April
the orchards bloom all night
and in the rise of light,
humid loam, swelling tulip buds
and red feathers come back
to the farmer's hill,
sing to each tree on the village lot

Green things push out, belief recurs,
hope, a bargain with the soil, takes root,
and for another season we can touch the land
and in the earth feel the sun return our heat

Making Way for the New Orchard

Uncles dig for grace
under the smoking roots
of the broken Gravenstein,
down inside its own drip line,
burning where it was felled

Their labor, penance,
silent among the brittle trees
left behind when the last Yankee
played out the last of the land

Grandfather gives no time to tears;
sentimental Italians stayed in the city,
so apples and thirty acres of garden crops
wear the family away like Russian
sandstone on a wet scythe

Fire sends plumes into the clouds.
Civil War orchards
abandoned by their settlers
melt back into the earth,
the ash mixing with hair
lockets, cobalt blue
bottles and the vertebrae
of the barn yard dog,

the velvet death dress
of the earlier farmer's wife,
the broken axe handles
thrown under the furthest row of trees
by the prior owner's drunken sons

Under the pooling smoke
father and the oldest hired man
are staking out straight rows
where they pray the next young
orchard will grow

Farm Inventory

Flanges and clevises,
dibbles and scythes,
bush and bog harrow,
double share plow,
grub axes, pick axes,
cold chisel, trowel,
hay tedder, cow tether,
needle-nose pliers, and dies,
nail punch, valve stems,
whetstones and crow bars,
box wrenches, spark testers,
hand-clippers, and knives.

Picking baskets,
radiator gaskets,
rip saws and files,
tire pump, chicken wire,
oil pan plugs,
wood screws and lug nuts,
pistons and wrist pins
and boxes of sockets.

Not even eight in the morning
and grandfather is calling for something
until some days by dark
you have touched every one
of them and he begins it again

Siphon pipe, drain cleaner,
plunger and snake,
swivel and auger,
basin and rake,
paraffin, grease gun,

Ear plugs and . . . . maul

Fire in the Wall

Blackening sod
meets broken stone
like old men's teeth
loose in purple gums

The bottom rocks hiss.
No one knows how they start,
these underground fires,
hot as the darkness at the core,
consuming humus unnoticed,
devouring roots, beetles, voles,
the bones of the family's last cow,
worms, the silt and sawdust
of the settlers' clear-cutting

Sometimes they smolder for days
while above the ground
boys fight wars with fallen fruit,
slipping in the slimy grass
and a gooseflesh
of half-flattened Macs

Until the tell-tale wisps,
rain-made steam, tendrils
of venting heat, pace the flame,

guide the fulgent rush of fire
out of the earth, up into the air
clawing for the random strand
of ivy vine, yellowed and dead

Catching it, the way death at sea
engulfs the sailor unaware,
flowering up the root into the leaf,
from the leaf into the rotten mossy oak
by the orchard wash, where the slangway
opens onto the road, not much more a road

Aspiring now to heaven
the light let loose from underground
burns its way to ascension
sucking the work sweat
of the huddled men
come to beat it down with brooms.

The words of father,
the tears of the workmen, the spit
from all their lips rising as steam

The oak blackens quickly
into a pyre of poison ivy,
spent nests, owl scat, forgotten beer bottles
hidden in its hollow by the hired man,
the flame consuming whatever it can,
trying in one roaring reach
to connect the soil under the loam
to the rim of space,
past bird, past bee, past anything
with roots or eyes or feet,
carrying something of the farm
into the last rarified breath of viable air
where the agitated exhalations
of men burn together
with the soot of Blue Jay beaks and claws

Grandfather at Mid-life

We remember him
on this day
his new black top coat,
nonchalant cigar
loose between his stony fingers,
Dutch Master smoke
curling up his sleeve

Father's father
dressed for death's obligation,
soft hat shadow
crossing the Italian angle
of his nose

Sons trying to imagine
him a child
playing innocent
among the lilies,
crying "mama, mama"
at the indolent approach of bees

Not their father
they decide,
never him
a child among the ankle skirts,

boy timid of the horse,
afraid to bathe alone
in the dark kitchen
under the oil lamp,
beside the rusty pump,
breezes raising the shade
at the single window,

A languid wing
trying to flap
as if it might lift
the cast-off Yankee house
and fly it to Providence, Boston
or Italy, anywhere
where the city light held back
this kind of night

This vision fits their uncle
the husband of the woman
who cut off all her hair
and wore his pants

It isn't grandfather
in the perfect coat,

him, now resolutely
sucking fire through
the still lit stogy stump
waiting for the mass to start

Crystal November biting
at his cheek and chin
all confidence,
almost insolence within

His existence
mapped inside the circumference
of the vestibule
of the family church
where they're saying
words for a sister
of his brother's wife,
the font beside him
where his boys were blessed,
the sky outside
framed in the aspiring door,
his farm beyond,
behind the village hedge
where they'll return tonight
to discover greater labor than before

Sailing Scythes

Seven men, chaff in the folds
of their burned necks,
father's helpers set to cut
all forty-seven acres of the farm
by hand with scythes

Seventeen days
of their peculiar dance,
half-hipped sway and step,
cut and step, sway and cut
straight into the choked alfalfa,
dense ragweed, rank clover,
blades forged in Austria
sliding soft under the grass
into the cool darkness
just above the yellow stems,
a sound like lake waves
rolling down the conga line
of beer swollen, sweat-sour men,
fanned out, careful, in a wedge
to clear swaths seven cutters wide

Curses rise - carbon breath
over the bowed heads,

each man's eyes on the hay,
oaths mingling with bees,
horse flies, fine dust that settles
into the hair, the eyes, the mouth
drying out every opening,
pollen coating a sheen of gold
onto each follicle and lash

At the last orchard
on the last day
with less than an acre left
euphoria and apples
pilfered from the Early Mac lot
swell together

Until, the uncut tuft
by the neighbor's wall
sits there, spiky, tall
shaggy head of truant land
abandoned by the cutters,
the last potential submission

Congratulations grow
to wild celebration,

seven men with blades
honed white,
medieval as sabers,
dangerous, mad enough,
to let fly their scythes at once,
seven hurtling wings
of wood and steel
soaring over the farm,
riding the wind
humming on the same harmonic
like avenging banshees
swarming at last

Under the Black Twig Tree

Expectations scattered, tattered dress torn,
thrown into the limbs of the Black Twig
by the door yard post, shoes lost in the droplets
under the drip line of the tree's umbrella

Down loving together on the sour floor of rotting fruit
Uncle risking yellow jacket rage amid the winey mash,
a fury of belts and pants and straps, right beside
the white, quiet brooding farm house, dark

Apples falling all around, and the wind on skin,
heart pumping, flash of white lobes, rushing breath a twin
of the dog's panting by bare legs, this passion sudden
as the howl of recognition, the clear scent of arousal

Until abrupt shocking fear of the backdoor light suddenly on
makes finding nylons crucial, retrieving socks and bra a panic,
the owl's unanticipated "who," the intimidating counterpoint,
who indeed, in the grass and stubble by the well at midnight?

Wet Clarinet

Slippery apple ladder rung
his perch,
the itinerant reed man
startles the pickers in the rain

Some Olneyville Benny Goodman
come to jam among the Gravensteins
here to juice the babes he met last night
at the hot jazz club downtown,
aroused, with blood red eyes

Women picking apples
to buy their cigarettes and gas
their night jobs at the weaving mill
just enough to make the rent, they
put down their baskets to lick their lips
primp their wettening hair

Droplets form on the apple faces
fill the dimples where the stems
go in and touch the hardened core

The music starts with no introduction,
wild as thistle; the cawing crow
answers from the cliff
beside the claw-raked bank
of father's pond,
stagnant with the sheen
from spray rig overflow

By each ladder the pickers
stand, a picket line of twisting
wool foot, country dawdlers,
who dream of dancing
in the orchard mud
but can't

While by the road
half way up
a half-picked tree
the melody made visible
comes in wild spurts
from the black wet clarinet

Sudden Flare Up

Swallows with their wings on fire
fly up from the burning brush
arcing through the orchard
rising into the winter-shriveled limbs

The boy runs for the corner
by the open cellar door
charcoal from the pitchfork
a dark chevron on his jacket

Father and his hung-over helper
freeze in the act of stoking
puckered bark and brittle sticks,
dead apple wood, into the inferno

The terrified birds cross in flight,
make a fatal X that hangs there
in the January air, to mark the hour
forever in the memories of the men

Only one, watching wide-eyed
from the window, hears the whimpers,
looks for her son,
hurting his eyes with dirty gloves

Father Eating, 2 a.m.

The kitchen
is dark and familiar,
gristle in the sink
floats almost white
beside bloated crusts
of bread.

Father sits in his boxer shorts,
his dinner chair pulled to the counter,
waiting with watery egg,
weak tea, gray toast
for the moon, the steady light,
his fingers feeling toward the bag
brown paper mouse
halfway off the saucer hiding
halfway round the cup.

Leaves of Grass face down
with the mail on the table,
his glasses there glinting
small darts of splinter light
reflected from the bedroom lamp
illuminating bare white sheets.

One hand rests his cheek,
leaves no room to smile,
no artifice possible in this sadness.
He keeps the spoon inside his cup,
winks one eye to drink
and hooks his thumb
behind the sterling silver shaft
to fend it off his nose.

It is November
and he's cold,
remembering farm darkness
in those first winters,
his long affair with words
a way of making space.

Boy mornings were moonlit too,
the beam diffused by window frost,
as thick as whiskers, coarse
and spirit white.
Now the glass is clear,
a frame waiting for the light
that might yet wash
across his hands, make a swath

the eye can follow
to the stove, the iron skillet
where it then will turn
the rime of grease to pearl
left in the aftermath
of frying one more meal,
one more dark hour breakfast,
eaten desperate for the dawn.

Father Climbs the Sky

Father climbs the sky
tree so black at night
it disappears into owls
and the rush of leaves
falling to the loam.

Needing stars in his hair,
the kitchen stove still
hot from the two o'clock eggs
and the gray tea of contrition,
he tries to escape apple gravity.

Farm armies crawl toward him
in the moonless dark hours,
white boots, flapping pants
and the strong strange steps
of men with shovels and an axe.

A fish could swim in the pool
of air that drips off the limbs
now when the bark is breathing,
replenishing the oxygen the sun
devours during the daylight hours.

There is only a moment before light
begins to tilt the time toward dawn,
to the weight of the others rising,
pulling the sky down around them,
wearing the clouds like hoods.

Until then Father climbs the sky,
his bare feet free, his song floating on gold.

At Last, Rain

Watching the water float
on the surface of the dirt
brown dust like coffee
unwilling to dissolve
after spending the summer
drying to a fine powder

It will, though, penetrate
and begin to make batter
of the loam and clay
where grandfather's dead
pepper plants hang their leaves
like withered gray lapels

The boys wanted to play baseball
today, the day no apples are sent
to market, no tomatoes are picked,
when the boys from town come

Grandfather, the killer of rats with a hoe
walks into the rain crying, the earth
running off his dirty arms like time

Love, Death, a Moment in a Cave

Twenty minutes down the road
meetings fill the buildings,
phones, like bees
thicken the air with sound.

In the cave that father found
on his father's father's farm
we make love on lichen
on top of rocky gneiss.

Two red tail hawks circling,
wait for soft fur to move.
Our moment swells against the stone.

One hawk folds wings and falls,
a bolt from the clouds,
diving
to a rendezvous
      with bone.

The Door Half Open

I want to speak through the door half open
to say I can hear them, the water running,
to tell them the angel in camouflage
and brown shoes is coming up the road
to sit on the trailer with cigarettes in his hand

I want to say the white beads of Mary
fast, before the frying starts and the bacon
drowns out the shouting and the clock.
The beads glow in the shadows and desires haven't stopped.
The men are arriving to wait for Father in the yard.

I need to speak through the door half open,
in the mirror, sister is breaking the eggs,
I will look for the one who never arrived,
who would make Italian noises and eat toast,
who couldn't stand the breaking glass either.

The door is cold and pine and cream
in color, the top panel cracked from a fist,
and the hinges squeal like voices the first owner
couldn't stifle, didn't take away when he left.
The orchards loose-barked and rotting
from lack of lime, two seasons of neglect,
the despair of empty whispers in the white steel bed.

I want to speak but the shade rolls up,
its spring failing, my words coiling,
lost in its black, retracting tail and sudden crack
against the window lintel, paint chips snowing
onto the stained bed, the words stuck by hunger
and fright, my throat closing to sponge.

Later – dry leaves scuttering by on the new tar road
seem to be talking, try to warn us of something,
lacking common language, but urgent, circling,
and no-one understands.

Little Red

It's the color
of the wool, pulled,
almost over your eyes
rubbing against you,
that's a distraction

Yet, it collects the devil's
pitchforks that might
penetrate your creamy cheek,
fends off the whipped
branch snapping unseen

Everyone needs some kind
of hood to hold tight,
a second skin to protect them
at the same time it marks
the path of their passage

Through the woods,
full of barbed wire briars,
over the river, bottomed
with jagged quartz, white,
a razor's mercy waiting

To grandmother's house
where even blood,
shared as it is,
shows teeth you can't trust,
runs red as the thing you think of as armor.

Seeing the Lion

The city cousin who came
to live here
thought the farm
had tigers
and those gazelles
they showed in the movies.
He wouldn't swim
with father and the men,
his dreams stalked by wet lions,
convinced he would find one
floating like the red rug
from Auntie's parlor
patterned with Asian dragons,
twisted fringe like whiskers,
the bulk of it rising and sinking
with the wind-whipped waves
on lower Donovan's Pond.
Afraid to put his Manton Avenue feet
in the rocky lake,
wearing his father's swim suit,
dry and faded from hanging in the sun
on the antenna of the Ford,
he worried the weed and mossy beach
looking for the shag head, yellow teeth

of the Serengeti beast, wishing it dead
wanting it alive to stare at,
seeing at last a red thing, pacing
on the far shore, the sun drying it,
his eyes straining to be sure.

The Backyard in October

Part way open, the door shines in the late light.
A child rehearses the anxious sound
of alarm behind the gray truck, outside
behind the gray truck where the pullet
is blinded by the sun, the sun frightening
the blue tick hound, one ear split by briars,
one eye runny as egg whites in hot water.

The child practices her fear shout and cries
at something, a cat claw surprise, white birds,
something her mother can't see, but tries to,
flying to the moss beside the well where her daughter
now laughs at the sun rousing two deer.

October light warms the walls of the coops
where father is checking the chickens for night,
the poultry odor of the brooder house floor clings
to his shoes, his shirt, the jingling pants he will leave
by the backyard door, the deer-troubled, daughter door.

The sun so low now it illuminates oil slick
under the transmission of the other woman's truck,
the truck parked by the bark pile against the barn,
where she's come to inseminate Herefords and goats,
the barn which grandfather wanted to burn.

In a breath, the sun will pull everything in behind it,
a drawstring closing a black satin bag, the rare light
giving up to darkness, the dark things it surrounds.

Late Plans to Escape

Rain he can't believe
plates the window blurry,
bullets of wet night, driven
ahead of the wind from the east

Mixed in are petals of April
apple blossoms, early this time,
and old leaves from October
gnarled into polio fists, clawing

Glass, old as the house,
through which father
and his midnight cousins,
his all day brother, stared

Their world enclosed by Gravenstein
trees and rows of Macs and Cortlands,
feared as soldiers advancing,
a fantasy later forgotten under the mud-stuck truck

He licks the storm water from his wrist
against the leaking sash, the aging house
losing itself into the weather, slaughter of leaves,
the dying trees still trying to get in

Morning in the Horse Meadow

Racing the horse
to the end of the water
an army of flies around
us, the apples under
our feet flattened to pomace.

Grandfather believes he has the key
to the clouds, the padlock
that secures the gate at the road
dangling from its round hasp,
his cheek a knot of tongue
and the bread from breakfast.

God and the saints brought him
to his knees in the dark before
the fire, yet the family was up,
bacon hanging sour in the hall,
hot peppers left in the pan all night,
an ambush for the eggs at dawn.

What might have been prayer
was a litany of cliffs and ruts, apple
maggots, and the Baldwin orchard,
a flood, three acres of rotting crops.

He rises all fury and veins
cursing the horse, the rider,
hating the lake, the neighbor,
his oaths a rosary of frustration,
willing the animal still, imposing
order on the anonymous chaos,
our stars receding into the new light.

Checking Out the Old House

Uncle's gun among the raincoats
in the front hall closet, crowbar
under the front step lattice with the cats.

Seeds in the pocket, in the rain
among the aspirin and the artichoke
leaves dried to horn, like old toenails.

Wind, thin as rice paper slides under
the porch door in endless freezing sheets,
ice on ankles stiff from inherited spurs.

Outside in half circles father succumbs
to the loosestrife wild in the yard, water
falling from his cap; high up a jay sees the rim.

This is the center to someone's world.
Below the cedar branches stretch trash bags
against the westerly wind, black circles of turbulence.

One sister's steps to the oak forgotten,
the tree now down in its own ring of dead
branches littered like mourners at a grave.

So much dusty wax waits, put aside in the cellar
for another season of canning the pears,
sealing the jars, the childish letters to her friend.

The thing underground has never come free,
resists the picks and shovels of the men
who still come back to look and cuff the earth.

Yet as secret as it was before the war, before
the war we thought was all we had to fear, a private
mist of sense cut loose from soul lurking out of reach.

The clothes line, held together by a thread
sags under a rotting pin, gray as a dead tooth
beginning to ache in the star-fed fury of your mouth.

The Axe and the Apples

In the Little Orchard to take down a tree.
Hit by lightning a Red Delicious split in two.
Father brings his Collins axe, water, a chunk of glass,
Old towels, a felling wedge and a pumice stone.

He knows the work, sets about it, quietly.
Using the stone with circular strokes,
Like someone applying makeup, he hones
The edge of the cold hard Collins blade,
Glasses its hardwood handle with slow strokes.

No swing wasted, he carves the trunk to chips
Uniform as a master cutting pumpkins,
The way a machine might leave them,
All done in little more than an hour's time.

Now smiling, he takes one of the towels,
And wipes sweat from his neck, rubs sap
From the axe with another, and then
He salvages the un-smashed, useful fruit.

He peels them with the axe, closer than mother
Does it with her paring knife, and eats his fill.

The Shape of Truth

Black furred goat
floats by the moon,
clouds weave up
from mountain river looms.

A shadow of my father
lies tethered against a ledge
in the center of a bog.

Careful, almost tender,
I climb astride the shape,
knees in the coarse dark hair,
elbow locked around the bearded throat.

Staying on his back
will take more than boyhood skill.
The clouds shift with every gust.

Like truth, my father seeks uncompromising forms.
Black goat alone in plum purple shrouds
eats tree top boughs, rears up, dissolves.

At Work

He grinds things.
With the glee of a boy
he pushes steel flange plates
into the wheel.
Sprays of fire
fly into his apron,
fluid stars light in his hair.
His audience of sparrows,
his dog, the spiders
come into the barn, go out.
Behind his black goggles his eyes
grow wild.
What joy is there
from disintegration
that he hops to the basket
to bring back a faucet,
a nail, a clevice to turn into dust.
At work he is perfectly happy.
He wears his shirt
laced with spark holes
more than a week.
At work he is perfectly happy.

Easy to Lose

The last black apple of November
beckons
the bird more than the farmer.
His eyes are apple sore,
illusions gone
he knows no further money is in store.

Two almost frozen snakes,
coiled under an overlooked box
at the Baldwin lot's far end,
drugged with their own cold blood
struggle to lift their heads
stare through the slats
at the ball with a stem
that this mountain of meat ignores
on his walk
to uncover them.

God's Man Among the MacIntosh

Come to find a job
picking apples
in the rain,
the frayed city worker
in low shoes,
dangles his milky shins
from the trailer tail

Father at the tractor wheel
pulls his crew out
to the Little Orchard,
shrugging October drizzle
from his collar

Once among the MacIntosh
the former tax collector's clerk
struggles up a picking ladder
shaped narrow, and pointed
like the window of a common church

Morning-after banter
drifts, tattering
among the limbs, the bark,
the yellow leaves

The woman just off
the night shift at the mill
rests her face, bleary
against the highest rung

School boy here
only for the day
barks at the orchard dog

The retired tailor
dumps his basket;
fruit spills, splitting
into the box,
apple shrapnel,
hand-picked pulp

The oldest man
breaks wind
naturally, as he walks
from the water bucket
to the boulder wall

Father puts his forehead
on the trailer rail,
kicks the ground

And now the clerk
begins his hymn

"What a friend we have in Jesus"
he scrapes it out
as grating as the winch
in the door yard well
"All our sins and strife to bear"

The picking stops
apples hang above
upstretched hands

The boy begins to laugh,
but stops
embarrassed by thought,
terrified by mercy

Prayer and Maggots

During mass the worms thrive
by the stone wall buttress
of the gothic steeple
where yellow tiger lilies rage

Taking time for church
takes time away from work
from the apple maggot wars,
the red-banded leaf roller purge.
They go anyway.

Every calyx is a star
each apple celestial
until scab and railroad flies
bring them back to earth.

Here prayer rarely mentions apples
or the battle to fight off blight,
diseases, and the fate of marriages
arranged by old men in the city.

Now something about the morning light,
the lilies, and an "Our Father"
comes from the slanted open

half-stained window by the altar,
the sound verging into silence
where the road takes over.

Father's hand rests on his mother's,
the missal sits in her lap, closed.

Back at the farm the parked spray-rig
leaks arsenate of lead and malathion
from loose bushings in the pump,
poisoning the earth below its oak belly,

waiting for grace
to release the men
so the small deaths
can begin again.

Fugue

　　　　I.

Cow tongue,
wet snake,
wire in the eye –

Wife at the prayer book,
a child behind the door.

The altars of alcohol
are draped for the night,
so home is the last resort.

One like this is ours.
Like this he comes
where we use the word,
wear the clothing,
make the sacrifice of time,
eat the soil of our birthright,
take down the bread and spoon,
sit in broken sofa silence,
delude the neighbor a little,
hide the wine,
sleep in the daylight,
hold onto our sides.

Here is where he comes
after his night,
after our worsening play,
where his shoes sit
brown and personal
under her comforter thread,
where his work shirt smells,
where orange rings
on the television
and ash in the carpet pile
say this is home.
It is here the sky
joins the earth,
here the silken
grip of muscle,
once so full, so free,
is forgotten
casually, sunk
in arguments over cereal,
school clothes and the cost of milk.

In another, earlier time
the rain was sugar
and the birds were happy
to be living in our trees.

II.

In the halo of smoke
her eyes have a glint
green as fish.

She whips her halter
in the face of our father
and dances over his coat.
The bar folk clap and cheer,
squint through the haze,
families out there in the dark,
odd as cheese in wooden boxes.

The jukebox throbs red, shiny,
its glass lips
humming vulgar tunes,
blood swelling the cells
of the dancers, close as dogs.

A whisky tenor grips the mike,
counterfeit passion
washes out to the crows
sitting like people
on stool after stool
in the back of the room.

Something is over,
it's clear, something is near
to the edge of rational grasp.
Something quavers in the rafters
where the feathers of vultures
have settled closer to claw.

    III.

His dreams are worse
than his shouting.
His bare feet
clicking long nails
into the floor,
our signal of anguish renewed.

Mother cooking bacon
and watering the azaleas
in the moment before dawn,
is a savior in bathrobe and clogs,
his food, his pain
the distractions
where life is reclaimed.

The Swallow in the Silo

In this upright tunnel
intoxicated by slow
sweet burning hay and corn,

dizzy as a Provençal
peasant four hundred
seasons earlier
in his round world, his circle
within the earth's great
            circle,

a swallow,
fascinated by a shaft of sunlight,
rides up it like a runway,
wings over
dropping like a late apple
dipping
like a dory in autumnal weather;

For centuries
the light outside moving
around the silo like a dial,
the dark bird twisting
after it,

unaware of marching armies,
rockets round and shaped
like silos, men in them
breaking away from earth,
the Sun a pathmark,
their hearts beating
fast as birds'

What Youth

What youth
was in this draggled bloom
leached off by rain at night,
bitter drink and broken teeth?

Where danced the cow man
and his sons, where in the gnarly woods,
swamp cabbage under their boots,
deer scat in the pools and fallen leaves?

No un-building of the walls, no
sad fingering of mother's lace
the war-cut uncle's cap, or father's comb
can will the weather
or stop the freezing wind

What youth
was lost in the sere petals
and tangle of the door yard,
what hope dried hard and useless
in the empty coops and earthless shale
of the lower garden lands?

Where now is the secret spring
that waters time and nothing else?

Morning Sun Rushes up Across the City

At the market
the sun rushes up across the city
between hill shag and tenement slant
to balance on the radio tower.

The old French peddler
looks hard for the poor fruit,
the oldest tomatoes.
His money is folded
around a Prince Albert can.

My friend is sleeping,
elbow hooked around the steering wheel,
knee against the floor shift
Even the breath of God would be stale here.

Not Often Seen or Found

The hired man doesn't think
horses think, or fish can feel.
He has never sailed, he's rowed,
but never flown or driven, walked
and thumbed and, as a boy, biked,
but never run, never taken a bus,
or been in jail; once he took a train.

He argues over the news and sports,
likes to drink and swim, dream of love.
He lives alone, can cook enough
to work in kitchens helping chefs
but he likes climbing trees, the certain feel
of Baldwin bark against his knees.
He is an apple orchard, apple-making man,
A dying breed from a stubborn faltering clan.

Breaking It

So much seems pointless
in the afternoon, in the ruts
wet between the Baldwins
and the valley of butternut squash

In the aftermath of the afternoon
I begged and kneeled in the mud
under the dying Elms behind the barn
where you walked me out to tell me

Our dream was rising into nothing
with the uncovering sun drawing
back the water the clouds had just let down
the day only long enough for more work

The night ahead too long to imagine
after the storm of what you told me broke
my awkward walk back to the apple job,
bruising Greenings and flattening Macs till dark.

Whole Piles of Brush

Whole piles of brush
drip water in their own
original patterns, no two
the same, no matter
whose hands stacked them,
which man gathered the ragged
limbs and suckers, broken tree
parts and errant alders growing
unwanted between the Macs

It is dark and pouring,
the low spots filling
deep with the late rain,
and they decide to burn
the brush piles, staggered
like drunken watchmen
among the rows in the lower lot

Regardless of their words
father and his brother make
a ritual without intention
of this night, this rare sunless
rite of smoldering fire at the far edge
among apple trellises and skeletons

It takes gasoline and no fear
of singed lashes and ears
to light something so drenched
on fire and sustain the clamor
of flames, make searing hot steam
when the heavens won't stop
suffocating everything outside
on this black and awful night

Sullen in the knee-deep truck rut
the two of them conspire
to use the gasoline to light
the spot they're standing,
make a small day in the darkness

Father's Typical Day

He makes the water can ring
against the outdoor faucet,
a tocsin warning to his cats.
Feeding them, watering the wheezing dog,
he walks on bones
that stab his heels.

A butterfly lights on his toe,
thin as leaf and yellow,
on the wet black rubber boot.

It rides his next two steps,
or does it lift his foot?

Weeds and ivy and brush
have been healing the land
down to a scar of open space.

He keeps the tractor to break a path;
it is his dead dog hearse.

Grandfather Kills a Rat by the Barn

Wattle-tugging knuckles
chicken killing hands,
grandfather laughs
around his wet perfecto
It's the rat's turn
webbed in by the wire cage,
the humane trap
looking like the framework
for a tiny dream blimp, the rat
crying with a pullet-hungry voice
its black, slick back
weaving back and forth
in the death basket
eyes two coal bullets
The pitch fork plunging
like a picador's lance
sweat flying
soaking the rat
all bloody black
the man and the animal
squealing barn-corner arias
in the lowering dusk.
I see it all night,
from the time he asks

for his slippers and water,
to the time the television goes off,
his arms rising, hands falling
like an angel, evil with palsy.

It is when I most try to know him
these nights, at the hassock, kneeling
to hand him the paper, hear his stories,
 grandmother in the pantry whistling,
baseball playing on the blue screen.

I hear the queer choir of noises all over again,
rage, fear, human voice blending with the rat's,
the wet tines puncturing fur, coming away red,
oaths and curses echoing from the hill
behind the house, returning to make a terrifying round.

Now though he speaks softly, familial, indulgent,
laughs, no sign on his face that he hears
what I can't stop hearing, or sees
anything but the ball game behind
the cloud of the day's last cigar.
It is dark and I am praying
he won't send me to put away
the pitchfork or wash the empty cage.

Fat With Water

Fat with water
the Bible
left outside, beside the pump
says nothing plain
about the argument
father and his father have begun.

Sicilian workers,
family, the two brown dogs,
drop down on the winey carpet
of apples underneath the Baldwin trees
to rest and wait
among the juice-drunk bees
to learn which way the afternoon will run.

Why Love is Like the Snow

It is white and goes on for acres and acres
covering everything it touches.
It softens a briar and thickens rope.
When it sticks to itself it grows.

In the right air you never see it coming
until it swarms all over your face
like white insects drawn toward gold.

When it hardens enough to bear their weight
two boys will cut from it the shape of a heart
and carry it in leather hats and tall boots
to the window where you can look and tell them
why love is like the snow
melting into their gloves, reddening their wrists
as they struggle to keep it from breaking.

The Blind Orchardist Refuses to Discuss the Day They Burned the Last of His Trees

He thinks himself
no more useful than a kite
memories of meals eaten
under the lattice
dominate his talk
hoof runes in the muck
by the cow barn
don't tell the history
of the land he left, unwilling.

He spurns tapes
and Braille,
pushes back.
His eyes climb up the wall
like flies. He smiles.

Perhaps
some neural ignition,
imagination's vision, has made him
picture ash rising to ride the wind
like the memory of a branch,
his orchard merging into clouds,
invisible at last.

At Father's House

I catch the curtain
climbing on the wind

Winter can be counted
on the wing,
wheeling toward the South outside
sour yellow
smells of newly rotting
leaves
mingle with the odor of
damp plaster in the air

Out this window
out this day
the shape of
daily boyhood play
dims beneath dark wind
and sepia skies

Who wants to keep apples,
corn, and farmer's art?
Who can bear
to suck the dirt
and love the work
that dries the heart?

Picking Peppers in the Dark, Fall Impending

Like a colored lantern, late-trimmed for night,
the television lights a square of kitchen
where chair, rug, dog, book, mug, pipe
create a nook for reclamation.

Yet, out into the sleeve of the dark,
like an arm practiced
in the camouflage donning of dusk,
Uncle runs across the acre of fodder
to the home garden near the piled loam
beside the river by the alder grove.

Our gloves from the afternoon
still grip the oak shafts of the wheelbarrow.
His boots slicked with dew
stand by the cold frame,
marking today's last step, tomorrow's first.

Moonlit peppers hang everywhere.
Uncle rushes to them,
squashes some to the ground
struggling after the flesh,
real and green and round.

Looking like small human hearts,
they throb when picked,
and, warm, they fit the hand,
as perfect as a traveler's lunch.

He eats obscenely of their meat,
gorges on sun and land and a year of rain.

Cold Baptism

This path, which is no more a path,
leads away from the farm and down
into the empty trees and briars.
Kite thin birds spiraling
in helix shapes and curls,
ride the howl of wind and pollen
behind each place he passes.

At the next wide bend
where the April rains fill
a freshet basin
the neighbor's girl
and the farmer's son,
years ago,
still children unaware,
went bare, all white
and cold with wonder,
their lower bodies
trembling under
the freezing brook
where they sat
beside the wild lilies
looking and trying to touch
until they could only

feel themselves in the chest
and neck and head,
sitting entranced
until her mother
called her name
in a banshee cry
and his father whistled
like he wanted
his work horse, Jim.
On the next ledge down
Lady Slippers grow in the ravine
where the farm wife's cow
slipped from the rocks
the pitchfork, icepick rain
freezing in the red fur,
here in the gravel
where she fell terrified
to force out the dying calf,
her bellowing cry fixed
in the farmer's heart forever,
the children's cold baptism yet to come.

Drunk Picker

Arms out
in a barrel grasp,
drunk's hug
covets the dress,
voluptuous with wind

Shambling gait
of the new hire
wandering from the shed
into the side yard
where mother's clothes
tango on the sagging line
while Astrachans rumble
from box to bin,
first of the new red crop

Each choice a gamble
when the help-wanted ads are answered;
violinists out of work,
parolees, teachers waiting,
and always the one-week
one-paycheck addicts,
high school boys, few serious,
some wives hoping for secret cash

Six weeks of intersecting
lives crossed by apples
and want, a harvest of need
staffed by chance
and father's best guesses

One lying now under
the dripping wash
singing Hank Williams songs
to bras and underwear,
his nose running on a rock

Which is Your Shadow

Hair will not grow on a scar,
grass will not grow on this grave.
The wind's signature
moves in blossoms and flowers
as if an angel were flying too near.

Could your prayer to connect us
be spelled in nailed joints of spruce
at the hen house,
orchards with their roots around stone?

The sound of carborundum
on steel seems to hang,
something real, like last notes
of music over the wild heresy
of ivy in the stubborn north lot
where obsession took you to mow.

Which is your shadow
among shadows in the Baldwin trees?

Old men who moth together at corners
in the Italian parks
don't see you in their reminiscence

any more, but under the packing shed
with your jumper and hat
there are eyes at twilight,
and the air has cheekbones.
Down in the square,
past the market,
the rain on Garibaldi's statue
is changing his expression to yours.

The edged tools at the farm will not wear out.
Apples in dreams come in a downpour.

It's certain your grandchildren
will search among cloud banks
for the shape of a face,
desperate for blessing;
they too will seek absolution,
the illusion of grace.

Finding the Algorithm of the Cove

Her white boat glows
in the magical foam
where fish by the inlet
make real the space
between the rocks
and the moss

If she moves without oar
or paddle, without rocking
and without wind
the trees cut the sun
into parallels of stain
that shine the water gold

Snakes swim
and the yellow
dog won't
and she knows the way
her sky-lit gunnel
will pass just so
over the dark, icy spring,
the slimy lure
lost by the brother,
fishing, home from war

Her dress trailing
the transom wicks
the lake up into her
thighs, the blue fabric
blackening, her smile
fixed as the compass
pointing to the one
spot in the cove
where the water
and the land
are truly neither

Believing in the rules
that much, she glides
toward the vanishing point
and the whole world
is outside of it and will
always be more wet, more dry
than where her body stops
in the one square foot
where air begins,
time turns into light
and this cove is solved and disappears

Last Mission

Somewhere in the sun-welded weeds
father's pliers lie,
rusted to a caked oxide
as unrecognizable as he is

Never stopped looking
for them, even when
his breath came in gulps
and he took a limb to walk

Out there where alders
are overtaking the orchard
and brambles lock the paths
he went each night while it was light

Poking at the grass and thickets
his foot sucked down by marshy ground
he was certain he could find them,
perfect for the small jobs, the hard places

Mother worried at the hour
and the strain, hoped the dogs
stayed with him, gripped by this thing
so treasured he couldn't let it go

Night on the Porch

For Laurence J. Sasso, Sr.

Driven to the chaise
by the failure in your chest
you seek air outside
the confines of the house,
flee the memories of youthful
running up and down the stairs.

You lie on your side at first,
then your back, heaving breaths
toward the orchard out beyond
the tattered screens where mosquitoes
try to match their micro bodies
with the pinholes in the mesh.

As you thrash, blood fights its way
through the thread-sized channels
in your tired veins, and you haltingly
talk about the fear at night and boy fights
with apples just across the street

In the dark on my cot beside you
I first turn away, but mostly I lie awake
and watch you struggle to breathe,

vigilant witness to the disbelief
as over and over your lungs
refuse to clear, you, the fastest
base-runner on every team you played for,
now turning the corner for home

The Light Across the Lake

Pin of incandescence
threading through the trees
a filament of memory
burning in the black November breeze

Uncle's vacant house
beyond the beach
the utter reach of recollection
flickering in the murk

No voice, no family noise
to drift across the night
from aunts and cousins
splashing adolescent feet
in the purple of the lake

Curtains gone,
chimney cold,
old tractor rusting
where the hay rake
stalled late one afternoon
when Nixon argued with DeGaulle
Dangling door claps
paint-poor frame,

bone hand demanding answer
from a toneless tambourine

Wild briars
wire off the threshold,
glass sands the floors,
wallpaper hangs like skin
burned from a vulture's wing

The sheds are empty
livestock long since lost
orchard rows are overgrown
gardens gone to moss
or covered with rank multiflora rose

At the center of it someone
keeps the barn light burning
and half-way up the lake
on the western hillside road
the semaphore of dots and dashes
made by leaves and limbs and clouds
blinks an indecipherable code

Digging Up a Hand

Wet slick clay
covers the shovel
rain runs under the hats
and down the collars

They are here
in the family plot
to open the land up
for another cousin,
trying to square
his last small space,
water pouring
into the grave

Apes in the haze
and fog of March
clawing down
amid the blackberry canes
and greening brambles
in a struggle to clear
what they failed to
clear between deaths
A thermos of coffee, already cold,
holds the gray, clay fingerprints
of father, the lead digger

Pruning tools
wrapped in canvas,
axes, saws, crow bars,
and a dozen gloves
sit in the cab
of the farm truck

One man is now
at the bottom,
mud sucking his boot,
two-handed clippers
working among a web
of maple tree roots
when, above him, next
to a panel of wet-rotted oak
and a boulder, the bones
of a hand, palm up, open
to funnel a rivulet onto his arm

He leaps from the trench
to run with the others
back to the kitchen,
hot soap and a jigger,
towels, the words of his wife
soft, slippery, like slurry

no one ready to return
to the chore

A morning of digging lost,
the day's farm labor delayed;
major misjudgment they call it,
half a day's work wasted
unearthing Aunt Mary
whose place never was well-marked.

Cold November

Boy view of the late sky
cloud hugging pine
on the mount of the pear,
almost forgotten.

Where now is that ache, that love,
the whistle and keen,
soft hum of mother
and her sisters
at the board with flour
water rolling into the sink,
the old oven burning their backs,
Zinnias filling pitchers and the bowls.

Where is the belt
the leather
father soaked with salt
from his own sweat
battering rock and furrow?

Television news and night
without moon or star,
the heart never far from here,
tears well up,
both foreign and fitting

as old photos cascade
onto the couch and chair

There's truth to the stream
of red leaves
blown like shot
against the clapboards,
the weather announcing
another hour of remorse

We are home,
if the family house
still fish-curtained
still wood-stove sour
is home.

Someone's wisdom shows
in the awning rolled
tight over the loft,
the drain pipe laid downhill,
grandfather's trellis bent back
and tied with cord

River rust and suet grease
on the maple board
behind his favorite seat

bring sparrows and peckers
to badger the wood with noise

Boy prayers lost in time
come back off the overhang
of the almost-mountain hills.

White limbed we climbed
so long ago with Robert Frost
and Whitman in our packs,
two loaves of Granny bread
and the hair net from Elaine,
stolen while she was in her bath.

Where can we go tonight
to buy some wine,
and eat a steak,
we'll have to chew too much

Where can we sit
in November and hear
nothing we have heard before,
and smoke in peace, and be contrite

Where can we be
when we can be no longer here?

Attributions

Under the Belly of the Fordson
Appeared in *The Olney Street Anthology*, published 1988 and in Volume IX, Number 1 of *Italian Americana*, Fall/Winter 1990.

Food from Home
Appeared in Volume XIV, Number 3 of the journal *Blue Unicorn*, published in June 1991. The piece also won third prize in *Blue Unicorn*'s 10th Annual Poetry Contest.

What Ever Rests?
Appeared under the title *What Can Ever Rest?* in the Fall 1981 issue of the journal *Sou'Wester*.

Girl on the Morning Horse
Appeared in Volume IV of the literary journal *Crosswinds*, published in May 2019.

Once Again April
Was selected for inclusion in the Eighth Annual Poetry & Art Exhibition and Publication as part of the 2020 Wickford Art Festival, Wickford, RI.

The Swallow in the Silo
Appeared in Volume 51 N2 of the journal *Thought: A Review of Culture and Idea*, published by Fordham University in 1976.

The Blind Orchardist Refuses to Discuss the Day They Burned the Last of His Trees
Appeared in the December 1987 issue of *Yankee Magazine*.

Cold Baptism – Excerpt From The Carpenter Walks
Cold Baptism is an excerpt from the opening section of *The Carpenter Walks*, an as yet unpublished nearly 2,000 word narrative poem.

Which is Your Shadow
Appeared under the title *Grandfather* in the Winter 1983 edition of *The Queen's Quarterly: A Canadian Review*.

Last Mission
Appeared under the title *Father's Mission* in the anthology *Regrets Only: Contemporary Poets on the Theme of Regret* published by Little Pear Press, 2006.